An Album of the American Indian

An Album of the

AMERICAN INDIAN

by Rosebud Yellow Robe
(Lacotawin)

Franklin Watts, Inc.
575 Lexington Avenue
New York, New York 10022

CONTENTS

An Album of the American Indian

INDIAN CULTURES OF LONG AGO

Introduction

About eleven thousand years ago, sometime after the end of the Ice Age, tribes of people came to the New World from Asia. They traveled across the Bering Strait into Alaska and by the fifteenth century they had spread throughout all of North and South America. These people were hunters, fishers, and food-gatherers. They wandered around the land to find food and they developed many cultures and many languages. By the time Christopher Columbus arrived in the New World there were over 13 million Indians there. The approximately one million Indians of North America lived in seven major areas: the Eastern Woodlands, the Southeast, the Plains, California, the Southwest, the Northwest Coast, and Alaska.

Eastern Woodlands

The Eastern Woodland Indians had many things to be thankful for. Deer, elk, bears, wild geese, and wild turkeys roamed the land. There were many rivers and lakes for fishing, and they could also fish along the seacoast. They harvested berries, fruit, nuts, and seeds. And they discovered that they could grow maize, or Indian corn, in the soil. The Eastern Woodland Indians became North America's first farmers. There were many Iroquoian-speaking tribes in the area. Around 1559 in New York, the Mohawk, Onondaga, Oneida, Cayuga, Seneca, and later, the Tuscarora, joined in a confederacy, or a loose grouping of tribes, to keep peace among themselves. This League of the Iroquois was begun by the Onondaga chief, Hiawatha.

Eastern Woodland Indians (THE NEW YORK PUBLIC LIBRARY)

Indian hunting deer
(THE BETTMANN ARCHIVE)

Indians hunting for beaver
(THE BETTMANN ARCHIVE)

Because the Iroquois tribes lived in the great woodlands they built their houses out of the bark and trunks of trees. These "longhouses" were often 100 feet long. They were heated by small fires inside, and since the longhouses had no windows, the smoke escaped through holes in the ceiling. Several families might live in one of these houses. A typical Iroquois village, usually consisting of twenty or more longhouses, also had a larger council house and a ceremonial dance circle. Farm fields surrounded the village, which was usually near a stream or lake. The most important crop was maize.

An Iroquois village
(HENRY E. HUNTINGTON LIBRARY)

A longhouse (MUSEUM OF THE AMERICAN INDIAN)

Council meeting inside a longhouse (NEW YORK STATE MUSEUM AND SCIENCE SERVICE)

The False Face Society of the Iroquois tribes wore masks when they performed dances to frighten away evil spirits that brought sickness to their people. Some in the False Face Society were medicine men. The Indians thought the medicine men were able to speak with the gods and knew special roots and herbs to use in curing illness. Their masks were carved from the wood of basswood trees. Then they were painted. Red was the most popular color. Often, long strands of black horsehair, and in modern times, hats, were added.

Modern Iroquois False Face Society dancers, Onondaga, New York State (AMERICAN MUSEUM OF NATURAL HISTORY)

Ojibwa Indians building canoes (AMERICAN MUSEUM OF NATURAL HISTORY)

Another type of Indian house found in the Eastern Woodlands region was the wigwam. It was round in shape and was made from the bark of the white birch tree. In the winter, bulrush mats were placed on the ground inside the wigwams to protect the Indians from the cold. White birch was also used to make canoes. The Chippewa and Ojibwa Indians were especially good at making wigwams and canoes. The Chippewa wore clothes and moccasins fashioned from deerskin. They wrapped their babies in fur and moss and strapped them to cradleboards which were tied to the mothers' backs.

7

Chippewa Indian women harvesting wild rice (AMERICAN MUSEUM OF NATURAL HISTORY)

The Chippewa Indians floated their birchbark canoes through lakes and ponds filled with wild rice. An Indian in the back of the canoe paddled along slowly. Indians up front pulled bunches of rice over the tip of the canoe and knocked the grains into the boat. On land, the outside covering of the rice was removed and the rice was dried and stored. The Chippewa lived in the Great Lakes region. In the winter they hunted the moose and the deer, the beaver and the otter. In the spring they tapped the maple trees that grew alongside the lakes and ponds for their sap. The sap was then cooked slowly to make sugar.

"The Moose Chase" by George de Forest Brush (SMITHSONIAN INSTITUTION)

An 1884 picture of an elm-bark lodge of the Sauk and Fox tribes. These Eastern Woodland Indians were pushed westward by the Chippewa. (SMITH-SONIAN INSTITUTION)

Southeast Indians

The best-known tribes of the Southeast were the Seminole, the Creek, the Cherokee, the Choctaw, the Chickasaw, and the Tuscarora. They lived in Florida, Georgia, Alabama, Mississippi, and parts of Louisiana and Tennessee. When an Indian reached adulthood in these tribes he was called a warrior. Those warriors who killed the most animals in the hunt, or enemies in battle, were respected the most. The bodies of the warriors were covered with tattoos. The tattooing was done by a village expert while the other members of the tribe chanted or sang songs. The tattooer pricked the skin of the warrior with a cactus spine needle or a flint, and put ink made from charred wood into the openings.

A Florida warrior
(AMERICAN MUSEUM OF NATURAL HISTORY)

Florida Indians hunting deer (AMERICAN MUSEUM OF NATURAL HISTORY)

All the Indian tribes in North America learned to make complete use of their surroundings. Deer were used for almost everything — the flesh for food, the hide for moccasins and clothes, and the antlers for tool handles. The cords and sinews that connected the muscles of the deer to the bones were used for thread with which to sew clothing, and the hooves were made into glue. The Florida Indians had a special way of hunting deer. They dressed themselves in deerskins so they could move very close to the animals.

Seminole Indians in a log canoe (THE BETTMANN ARCHIVE)

The Seminole Indians lived on the richest lands in Georgia. Rivers, ponds, and creeks were filled with fish. The woods were filled with berries and fruit; the soil was good for growing squash and melons. As the white man settled in Georgia, the Seminole were forced into Florida, which was then Spanish territory. They lived there in peace. But when the Seminole gave food and shelter to Negro slaves escaping from Southern plantations into Florida, United States Government troops invaded this Indian nation with whom they were at peace. When Spain sold Florida to the United States in 1819, many Seminole fled to the Everglades. They were proud people and fought in the swamps for survival.

Plains Indians

The major tribes of the Plains area were the Sioux, Pawnee,
Cheyenne, Blackfoot, Shoshoni, and Mandan. Buffalo herds
roamed the flatland looking for the rich grass that grew there.
Winters on the Plains were cold. In Mandan villages, homes
were made from earth. To keep warm, the Plains Indians
wore fur robes, with the fur placed on the inside. The outside hide was decorated with beautiful designs in earth
colors. A popular pastime of the Indians on the Plains was
the hoop and pole game. The Sioux tossed a hoop into the
air and caught it on a forked pole as it came down; the Mandan sometimes rolled a hoop along the ground and speared
it on the run.

Mandan winter village (SMITHSONIAN INSTITUTION)

Women poling bullboats. A Mandan village in the background. (SMITHSONIAN INSTITUTION)

The Mandan lived in the Dakotas long before the Sioux Indians moved there. Lewis and Clark, the famous explorers, wrote about the Mandan tribe when they visited them in 1804. The earth lodges the Mandan built were wooden frames lined with wicker and mats, on top of which was packed wet earth. This earth dried to form a low, round house. These houses were able to stand up under the strong winds on the plains. The Mandan did not have enough wood to build canoes. Instead they made round boats of skins, called bullboats. When the Sioux migrated from the east to the Dakotas they saw the Mandan bullboats for the first time. They thought it would be a good idea to turn the bullboats upside down and place them over the opening at the top of their tepees, to keep out the water when it rained.

14

A Mandan chief's lodge was spacious. Sometimes his favorite horses and dogs lived in the lodge with the family during the cold winter months. In some tribes, when the chief died, his horse was tied to the high platform on which the chief's body rested (scaffold burial) and was killed. The Mandan men sat on fur mats in the lodge and smoked the calumet, a long-stemmed pipe used by many of the Indian tribes. The calumet was called a peace pipe because the Indians smoked it when they were trying to settle disagreements. The chief often leaned against a backrest made of reeds. Clothing and moccasins hung over a wooden bar to dry in the sun.

A Mandan lodge (SMITHSONIAN INSTITUTION)

The Plains tribes got their food, clothing, tools — and even their houses — from the wild buffalo. The tepee, a typical Plains Indian home, was made by placing poles in a circle and bringing them together near the top. This form was covered with buffalo skins sewn to form a single piece. The tepee was held in place by wooden pins and ground pegs. Tribes moved their camps often in search of bigger herds, and the tepee was an excellent movable house.

At first the Plains Indians frightened the buffalo into log stockades and killed them there. Later, after they had bought horses from the Southwest Indians, they rode swiftly around the buffalo, frightening them with shouts and killing them with spears, bows and arrows, or guns they bought from white traders.

Buffalo hunt (SMITHSONIAN INSTITUTION)

Buffalo dance, after a drawing by Carl Bodmer (SMITHSONIAN INSTITUTION)

Since buffalo meat was their primary food, a successful buffalo
hunt was necessary for the Indians' survival. They cut the
buffalo meat into thin strips, dried them in the sun, smoked
them, and mixed them with dried berries and fat. The result
was pemmican, a food that was easy to keep and carry.
The day before the hunt, a buffalo dance was performed. This
ceremonial dance foretold the success of the hunt. The dancers dressed themselves in buffalo heads and tails, moccasins,
and necklaces of bear and eagle claws. They painted their
bodies, and sometimes even painted their horses. Rattles,
drums, and singing accompanied the dancers' movements.

17

Indians hunting the buffalo (SMITHSONIAN INSTITUTION)

"Buffalo Chase-Surround" by George Catlin (SMITHSONIAN INSTITUTION)

Painting on buffalo skins
(SMITHSONIAN INSTITUTION)

Buffalo skins were often painted with stories of the important events of an Indian chief's life. Before Sequoya invented the Cherokee alphabet, the Indian had no written language. Pictures told the history of a tribe. Different tribes spoke different languages, and so the Indians learned to speak to one another by using a sign language. At night, fires were built on high hills to communicate warnings. Long-distance smoke signals were also used to exchange messages. During the day, when smoke could be seen, blanket signals were used. The signals were made by throwing a blanket over a smoldering fire to catch the smoke. When the blanket was taken away a puff of smoke rose toward the sky.

19

"Medicine Man in Curing Costume" by
George Catlin (SMITHSONIAN INSTITUTION)

There were a few men, and sometimes a few women, in every
Indian tribe who were believed to have supernatural powers.
It was thought that they had received at birth, or through
dreams, powers from the gods to cure disease. The Plains
Indian medicine man was feared as well as respected. He
carried a bundle of important objects that were used in his
healing ceremonies. If a patient did not get well, the medicine man sometimes said that an evil spirit was the cause of
the disease. If too many people died, it might be felt that the
medicine man himself was an evil spirit, and he was put to
death.

The conelike tepee was a very good home for the Indians who had to move about often. It could easily be taken apart and put together again by one person. It was kept warm inside by a dew cloth, or inner lining, and a fire in the middle. The inner hanging was decorated with beautiful geometric designs or with paintings of the family history.

When the Indians moved their camp, tepee poles were used to make the travois, a sledge drawn by an animal. A platform was attached to the tepee poles which were then tied to a horse that carried belongings, children, old people, or the sick. Before the Dakota Indians had horses, dogs dragged the travois.

Woman seated on a horse drawing a travois on which there are two children and belongings. The horse is a white man's horse, not an Indian pony.
(SMITHSONIAN INSTITUTION)

"Sioux Chief" by Frederick Remington, 1901 (THE BETTMANN ARCHIVE)

One of the greatest Indian tribes of all was the Sioux. The Algonkin name "Sioux," meaning "snake," was given to them by their enemies, the French. They called themselves Lacota-oyate, "a great nation." Other tribes copied their warbonnets, tomahawks, bows and arrows, and their fine horsemanship. When the Sioux discovered the horses of the Spanish settlers in the Southwest, they learned how to travel miles and miles over the plains, riding bareback. As warriors, they learned to ride leaning over one side of a horse, using the horse's body as a shield against enemy attack. They called the buffalo "Tatanka" — and he was looked upon as a sacred gift from "Wakan tanka," the Great Spirit. The Sioux hunted the buffalo through South Dakota, Nebraska, Montana, and Wyoming.

Indians of the Plains staging a horse race (THE BETTMANN ARCHIVE)

Sioux warriors (THE BETTMANN ARCHIVE)

California Indians

Over 150,000 Indians lived in California long ago. They were divided into forty tribes, and they spoke twenty different languages. They used tule reeds to make thatched homes and open-sided roof shelters to protect themselves from the hot sun. They depended on acorns and seeds for most of their food. When gold was discovered at Sutter's Mill in 1848, the Indians were forced, by a series of eighteen treaties called the Barbour Treaties, to give up their rights to 75 million acres of land. White settlers stole Indian children from their families and sold them to other white settlers as laborers in Southern California. No longer were acorns and seeds plentiful, for the settlers harvested them and fed them to their hogs. Thousands of Indians died from hunger and disease, and the population shrank. Today only 7,000 California Indians are living in the state.

Homelife of the Indians of California (AMERICAN MUSEUM OF NATURAL HISTORY)

Coronado on his search for the Seven Cities of Cibola (AMERICAN MUSEUM OF NATURAL HISTORY)

Indians of the Southwest

The Spanish conquered Mexico and Peru in the 1500's. The Spanish explorer Coronado set out from Mexico in 1540 in search of the fabled Seven Cities of Cibola which he believed to be filled with silver, gold, and jewels. He found the Pueblo Indians instead. The Pueblo tribes of the Southwest were the Hopi, Navaho, Zuni, and the Apache. The Spanish picked an Indian governor for each Pueblo tribe and gave him a gold-headed cane as a symbol of his office. President Lincoln continued this practice when treaties were signed between the Pueblos and the United States.

25

A Hopi pueblo (PERRY PICTURES)

A pueblo was a type of village built by the Indians of the Southwest. Its buildings were placed in a receding terrace formation and each one housed a number of families. The houses were flat-roofed and built of stone or clay. They were America's first apartment houses. Some of the houses were four stories high, and some had over five hundred rooms. The people reached their homes by climbing up ladders placed on the outside of the larger buildings. A room below the ground was special. It was called a kiva and was used for religious ceremonies and social meetings. When other tribes raided a village, the Pueblo Indians pulled up their ladders and the enemy had a hard time getting in.

26

Animals were scarce in the Southwest and most Indian tribes relied on farming for their food. Some deer, rabbits, wild sheep, gophers, wild turkeys, and lizards could be caught; but corn, beans, and pumpkins served as the main foods. Corn was ground into meal and made into a mush or into "piki," a baked, thin, crisp cake. The Indian women, carrying baskets, left their villages in search of giant cactus fruit, acorns, and seeds. In ceremonial dances, the Indians asked their gods for rain and for good harvests. The Walpi Indians were especially famous for their snake dances, in which the dancers carried live rattlesnakes in their hands.

The green corn dance of the Jemez Indians (THE BETTMANN ARCHIVE)

Navaho women weaving a rug (UNION PACIFIC RAILROAD PHOTO)

One of the largest tribes in the United States is the Navaho tribe. Navaho is the name the Spanish gave to the tribe. They called themselves "Dine," meaning "the people." When the Spaniards came to the Southwest they introduced the Indians to the sheep and horses that they had brought with them from Europe. The horses were traded to the Plains Indians, who, because of them, became famous hunters and warriors. From the soft wool of the sheep the Navaho made rugs, blankets, belts, and dresses. The Navaho became known for their weaving skills and for their beautiful designs. They used natural dyes that they made from vegetables.

28

Pacific Northwest Indians

The Pacific Northwest Coast Indians fished for salmon and traded their fish with hunting tribes for furs. They fished with hooks, lines, nets, and spears, and they built log dams to trap the fish. They harpooned whales in the ocean and cooked the blubber down into oil which was used for fuel, for light, and to preserve food. Many of the tribes built large homes from red cedar trees. Several families lived in one house, separated from each other by mats that hung from the rafters. Excellent canoes, totem poles that traced the history of a family, ceremonial masks, carved boxes and buckets, dishes, clothes, mats, ropes, and many other objects were also made from the cedar and its bark. The major tribes of the area were the Haida, Kwakiutl, Tlingit, Tsimshian, and Chinook.

A Northwest Coast house built, painted, and carved by the famous Indian artist Lelooska (U.S. DEPARTMENT OF THE INTERIOR)

29

A Chilkat blanket of the Tlingit tribe (SMITHSONIAN INSTITUTION)

The Indians of the Northwest held big feasts called "potlatches" to which they invited guests from many other tribes. "Potlatch" is a Chinook Indian word meaning "to give." At the feast, which might be held to celebrate a wedding or the birth of a child, each guest was given a gift. A guest would then return the favor by inviting the host to his own potlatch where he gave away even more expensive gifts. A guest might receive furs, food, beautifully carved boxes, or blankets. Only rarely was the Chilkat blanket given away. The Chilkat blanket is a wonderful example of weaving, fringing, and design. It was worn as a cape by the chiefs of the tribe and was made from the wool of the mountain goat, mixed with shredded cedar. The Northwest Indians often wove cedar bark into their clothing.

Alaskan Indians

At one time it was believed that the Alaskan Indians came from Asia by way of the Bering Strait. Now anthropologists believe that the Northern Indian came from Greenland. When a Danish captain discovered Alaska in 1741 he found the Eskimo, Tlingit, and Aleut Indians. These people were fishermen and hunters who moved their homes often to follow the game and the fish as the seasons changed. At first they ate raw fish but later they learned to boil their food in Tlingit baskets. Like all Indian tribes they learned to make use of everything around them. They used animal skins, wood, bark, bones, and even ice blocks, to make their houses.

Indian dance at Unalakleet, Norton Sound, Alaska (THE BETTMANN ARCHIVE)

COMING OF THE WHITE MAN

When Christopher Columbus landed in the West Indies he thought he had found India. He called the people he found there "indios" and gradually all the native peoples of America came to be known as Indians. Columbus was not the first European to come to the New World — the Norsemen arrived in New England five hundred years earlier. After Columbus, however, more and more Europeans were to come to the New World. The Indians along the Eastern Coast were the first to meet the Europeans. They were friendly and helped the first settlers make their homes. The Pilgrims could not have survived without the help of the Indians who showed them how to plant corn and how to hunt and fish.

The landing of Columbus (AMERICAN MUSEUM OF NATURAL HISTORY)

The marriage of Pocahontas, April, 1614, in the church at Jamestown (PERRY PICTURES)

Powhatan, chief of the powerful Algonkin Confederacy, welcomed the white settlers of the Jamestown Colony in 1607. He taught them the ways of the forest, how to hunt and fish, and how to plant their own corn. A British settler, Captain John Smith, wrote in his volume on the history of Virginia that when he was discovered exploring on Indian property, Powhatan ordered him beheaded. Smith said that Powhatan's daughter Pocahontas saved his life by throwing herself over his body as he was about to be executed. In 1613, Pocahontas was captured by the British and taken to Jamestown where she was held as a hostage to insure the good behavior of the Indians. There she met and married James Rolfe, an Englishman. She was renamed Lady Rebecca and went to England with her husband. Because of his daughter's marriage, Powhatan kept peace with the English settlers until his death in 1618.

When Henry Hudson discovered the Hudson River in 1609 he was attacked by the Wappinger Indians. However, as more and more Europeans came to the New Land, the Indians were forced into friendly contact with them. The Spanish arrived in Florida in 1513, the French explored the St. Lawrence Valley in Canada in 1535, and the English began to settle along the Atlantic Coast. Peter Minuit, a Dutchman, bought Manhattan Island from the Indians in 1626 for 60 guilders (about $24.00) and some trinkets. Roger Williams was aided by the Indians when he was sent away from Salem, Massachusetts, because of his religious beliefs. With their help he founded Rhode Island.

The landing of Roger Williams on Rhode Island (PERRY PICTURES)

John Eliot preaching to the Indians
(AMERICAN MUSEUM OF NATURAL HISTORY)

John Eliot was a missionary to the Indians in Massachusetts, and in 1646 he began a system of Indian town communities. With the help of his Indian converts and his sons, Eliot translated the Bible into the Algonkin language in 1663. Eliot was a good friend to the Algonkin people, but he also spread the idea that to "educate" the Indian meant to replace his way of life with the white man's. This attitude damaged the Indian's respect for himself and his own culture and is perhaps responsible for the conflict between the Indian and the white man which continues to this very day. Eventually, Harvard and Dartmouth colleges were founded for the education of the Indian. But the Indians who returned from these colleges to their tribes were looked down upon, for they were now ignorant of the ways of living in the forest.

35

Colonial villages grew rapidly. When the white man began to farm on Indian lands, trouble between the two groups grew. In the early 1600's Chief Massasoit of the Wampanoag tribe had given great amounts of food and land to the Plymouth Colony and was friendly to the white man. After he died, his son Philip became chief. Philip was also friendly to the white man, and in 1671, he even agreed to hand over the Indians' guns to the Colonists. "King Philip's War" began, however, when white settlers continued to move onto more and more Indian lands and a few white men and Indians were murdered. King Philip and other great Indian alliances fought against the Colonists. At first they were victorious, but the Indians lost the war when some tribes betrayed Philip and surrendered. Philip was run down in the Assowamset Swamp and shot. His wife and nine-year-old son were sold into West Indian slavery.

King Philip, son of Massasoit. Killed in battle on August 12, 1676. (SMITHSONIAN INSTITUTION)

The Indian and the Colonist struggle for possession of the land in the early days of America (THE BETTMANN ARCHIVE)

The struggle between the Indians and the settlers became worse. Sometimes the Indians, hiding behind trees and rocks, surprised their enemy in the woods. They were trained to fight with bow and arrow, hatchet, and knife. Other times they surrounded a settlement and attacked over and over again until they had killed all the settlers. On March 22, 1622, Opechancanough, the leader of the Indian nations of Virginia, made a major surprise attack on many English settlements. The bloodshed was so terrible that it was bitterly remembered by the Colonists for years. In 1675, settlers on the Virginia frontier were helpless against Indian attacks. The Government would do nothing to protect them. Nathaniel Bacon defied the Colonial Government and led three hundred volunteers to attack the Indians in their own camps.

37

Sacagawea guiding Lewis and Clark through the Rocky Mountains (THE BETTMANN ARCHIVE)

An attempt to build friendly relations with the Indian tribes was made in 1803–1806 by Lewis and Clark. President Jefferson gave the two men a "Jefferson peace medal" to present to the Indian chiefs of the Louisiana Territory. On their trips, Lewis and Clark were helped by Sacagawea, the sixteen-year-old Indian wife of their interpreter. When their boat overturned on the Missouri River, Sacagawea saved the records and instruments. When they came to the village of her people, she asked the chief to give Lewis and Clark horses and food. With these new supplies they were able to continue on their way. On the return trip, when they became lost, Sacagawea guided them through the mountain passes of Montana.

THE INDIAN WARS

The Indian wars began in the early 1600's and continued up to the 1900's. They were fought because the Indians did not want the white man to take over their land. The Indians respected and loved the land; it was a part of each and every one of them. They did not cut down great forests or kill game except for what they needed. They believed that Wakan tanka, "the Great Spirit," had given them this gift of land and food for everyone to share. When they signed treaties they believed they were only allowing the white settlers to use the land, not to keep it forever. In 1682 the Algonkins made a famous peace treaty with William Penn. They gave Penn a wampum belt showing an Indian and a white man clasping hands in friendship. As long as Penn lived, the peace treaty was kept. But William Penn's was one of the last peace treaties to be kept by the white man.

Penn's treaty with the Indians (PENNSYLVANIA ACADEMY OF FINE ARTS)

In his greed for land, the white man broke treaty after treaty. There was violence and massacre on both sides. The Indians made surprise attacks on settlers' homes and on well-fortified stockades. The English settlers fought back. The settlers became involved in a war with the Pequot tribe in 1637 and made a surprise attack on the Indians' main fort near the Mystic River in Connecticut. Probably six hundred Pequot men, women, and children were shot down while trying to escape. Their defeat was so overwhelming that they were forced to separate into small groups and leave Connecticut.

The massacre of the Pequot (THE BETTMANN ARCHIVE)

Indians attack settlers at Wilkesbarre (THE BETTMANN ARCHIVE)

Indians attack Fort Mimms (THE BETTMANN ARCHIVE)

The French and Indian War was really the French and English War. The two countries were fighting for the possession of North America and for profits in the great fur trade. The Indians were divided. The Iroquois fought along with the British. The other Algonkin tribes helped the French. In 1753, French traders offered gifts to the Indians to keep their goodwill. Indians helped to defeat the British General Braddock at Fort Duquesne along the Ohio River. But when the British General Wolfe captured Quebec, the war was won and the French were defeated. The Treaty of Paris gave Canada, Florida, and all of the French possessions west of the Mississippi to the British.

The Iroquois battle the French during the French and Indian War (THE BETTMANN ARCHIVE)

Chief Cornplanter (left) and Chief Red Jacket (right) (SMITHSONIAN INSTITUTION)

During the American Revolution many Indians joined the English in their fight against the Colonists. Chief Cornplanter, a great Seneca chief, was one. After the Revolution, Cornplanter made a peace treaty with George Washington which set aside reservations for the Indians in New York State. Another Indian warrior who fought in the Revolutionary War was Red Jacket, so named because he fought with the British soldiers who wore red coats. Later Red Jacket joined the American Army, and fought against the British in the War of 1812. He became a great spokesman of his people, uniting them to defend their customs and their lands.

The Greenville Treaty of 1795 which protected Indian lands from the white man was broken when American settlers spread north and west of the treaty line into Indian territory. Chief Tecumseh of the Shawnee tribe stood firmly against this western expansion. He formed a great confederacy of all the western and southern tribes. In 1811, when he was away trying to gain support from other tribes, one of his men allowed himself to be stirred up into a fight with U.S. troops under General William Henry Harrison at Tippecanoe. Tecumseh returned to find his people defeated. He joined the British as a brigadier general in the War of 1812, commanding both Indian and white soldiers. Tecumseh died at the Bloody Battle of the Thames, which signaled the end of the war. With him died his last hope for his people and their land.

General William Henry Harrison at the time of the Indian wars, pictured with Tecumseh. Harrison later became the ninth President of the United States (THE BETTMANN ARCHIVE)

44

Osceola, chief of the Seminole
(THE BETTMANN ARCHIVE)

Chief Osceola, who was of Creek ancestry, came to the aid of the Seminole in 1817. He led them in the first Seminole War against General Andrew Jackson. The U.S. Army wanted to clear Florida land of the Indians but could not bring Osceola to defeat. In 1832, some of the Seminole had, under pressure, signed a treaty which would force them to leave their Florida lands in three years. But when the three years were up, the Seminole did not want to leave their homes. So the second Seminole War began. Osceola hid the women and children, the sick and the aged, in the Florida swamps. He began a guerrilla warfare campaign that lasted for seven years. When the United States Army asked to meet with him under a flag of truce, he was captured. He died in prison a short time later. The Seminole surrendered and were moved to reservations in the west.

45

The Cherokee, Chickasaw, Choctaw, Creek, and Seminole were called the "five civilized tribes" because they made so much progress in the nineteenth century in learning how to read and write. The inventor of the first written language among all tribes was Sequoya, a Cherokee genius. Sequoya invented the Cherokee alphabet in 1821 and was given a medal by the Cherokee National Council for his great gift. In 1838, gold was found on the lands of the five civilized tribes and the Indians were driven from their homes. Four thousand Indians died on the march which became known in history as the "Trail of Tears."

Sequoya
(SMITHSONIAN INSTITUTION)

*"Our new Indian Policy. Which is the Savage?"—
from a cartoon criticizing the outrages committed
against the Indians by the United States Army in
1873* (THE BETTMANN ARCHIVE)

War between the white man and the Indian raged again and
again as the country expanded westward. Texas joined the
Union in 1845, and in 1848 the peace treaty ending the
Mexican War extended the southwestern region of the country to the Pacific Coast. The discovery of gold created a rush
of wagon trains along the Oregon and Mormon trails. As
they headed west, the settlers faced angry Indian tribes.
Pledges made to the Indians had been broken time and time
again. Now the Government sent its cavalry out to defend the
settlers and to make surprise attacks on peaceful Indian
camps. Scalping was common on both sides.

47

Cavalry coming to the rescue of a wagon train attacked by Indians (THE BETTMANN ARCHIVE)

The cavalry attacks an Indian camp at dawn (THE BETTMANN ARCHIVE)

A reenactment of the "long walk" (NEW MEXICO MAGAZINE)

The white man continued to take away the Indian's hunting grounds and to convert them into farms and towns for his own use. He killed most of the buffalo on which many tribes depended for food. Some greedy hunters wanted only the hides to sell. The white man had more guns than the Indian, including the newly developed breech-loading gun for more rapid fire. In 1863 Colonel Kit Carson, an American scout and frontiersman, rounded up 8,000 Navaho Indians, destroying their sheep and taking their horses. The Indians were forced to take a "long walk" from Fort Defiance, Arizona, into exile at Fort Sumner, New Mexico. They were imprisoned for five years. Then the government sent 8,000 of these half-starved people on the "long walk" back to Arizona and to parts of New Mexico that were unwanted by the white man.

Fighting between the Apache and U.S. Government troops ended with the surrender of the Chiricahua Apache leader Geronimo. Geronimo was a very brave and clever warrior who had become famous for his fights against the Government in the Sierra Madre Mountains. When the Chiricahua Apaches were forced by the Army to move to the San Carlos Reservation in Arizona, Geronimo escaped to Mexico. He was captured but made many raids against the U.S. Army for the next ten years. In 1886 Geronimo surrendered, and his two dozen warriors and their families were imprisoned in Florida. Geronimo's fearless courage inspired U.S. paratroopers in World War II to shout "Geronimo!" as they jumped from their planes into battle.

Geronimo (1829-1909)
(SMITHSONIAN INSTITUTION)

Fort Sill, 1871 (THE BETTMANN ARCHIVE)

Fort Sill was a large United States military post and reservation located on Medicine Bluff Creek in Comanche Country, Oklahoma. Many Army campaigns against the Wichita, Kiowa, Comanche, and Apache Indians were planned at Fort Sill. The United States Cavalry was stationed there, and they often went out from the fort to chase bands of hostile Indians who were running off with large numbers of horses and mules belonging to the white settlers. In 1871, President Ulysses S. Grant ordered Fort Sill to set aside 23,040 acres as a reservation and agricultural settlement for the Indians. The last group to arrive were the Chiracahua Apaches who had been sent to Florida after their surrender to the white man. Many Chiracahua had died of disease in Florida and the War Department decided that the climate at Fort Sill was better for them.

General George A. Custer with Indian scouts (THE BETTMANN ARCHIVE)

The Seventh Cavalry under Lieutenant Colonel George A. Custer was sent to Fort Rice in the Dakotas to protect the men who were building the Northern Pacific Railroad from Indian attack. Custer was then ordered to locate the Sioux, who had gathered a force of 4,000 warriors at the Little Bighorn River in southern Montana. He was told not to attack when he found them, but to send back to the fort for more soldiers. But Custer wanted to win a major victory and become famous. When he reached the Little Bighorn Valley, he did not listen to the warnings of his scouts. He decided to attack. One of his divisions was forced to retreat, another was unable to come to his aid. Sitting Bull, one of the major Sioux chiefs, surrounded Custer and wiped out his entire command of 264 men.

The Nez Percé Indians of Oregon had long been friends of the white man. But as settlers and miners moved west seeking gold, they asked the Government to change the treaty of 1855 and force the Indians onto a smaller reservation. Chief Thunder-on-the-Mountain, called Joseph by the white man, tried to protect Indian lands. Angry Nez Percé Indians killed settlers and miners, and the Government declared war against them. Joseph was a brave fighter and eventually he was forced to retreat. Only fifty miles from the Canadian border his band of warriors, women, and children was cut off by Colonel Nelson A. Miles. At the time of his surrender Joseph said: "Hear me, my chiefs, I am tired. My heart is sick and sad. From where the sun now stands, I will fight no more."

Chief Joseph (1840-1904)
(MUSEUM OF THE AMERICAN INDIAN)

Chief Joseph surrendering to General Miles on October 5, 1877 (THE BETTMANN ARCHIVE)

The "Sitting Bull" Council at Fort Walsh, British Territory in Canada, October, 1877. At this meeting, American commissioners tried to convince Sitting Bull and the Sioux to return to the United States and surrender. Sitting Bull did not accept their terms. (THE BETTMANN ARCHIVE)

Sitting Bull, a Hunkpapa Sioux, was one of the most famous of all Indian chiefs. His people lived in the Black Hills of South Dakota, which the United States promised would never be settled by white men. When gold was found there, the promise was broken. Chiefs Sitting Bull and Crazy Horse were angered. They attacked and defeated Custer at the Battle of the Little Bighorn. The Government continued to chase after Sitting Bull. He fled to Canada, but when he returned, he was taken prisoner and sent to live on a reservation. In the 1890's Sitting Bull led the religious "Ghost Dance" movement that excited the Indians to dance and pray for a return of the land they had lost. The Government tried to stop the dance movement. When the Indians refused, Sitting Bull was arrested. He was shot by the Indian police during the arrest struggle.

Sitting Bull (1834-1890)
(SMITHSONIAN INSTITUTION)

Spotted Tail was one of the many Brule Sioux chiefs to sign a treaty in 1868 giving the white man part of South Dakota. But as in so many other cases, the treaty was broken when gold was found in the Black Hills and settlers came onto Indian territory. Some of the Indians roamed the land in hostile bands, attacking the settlers who had broken the treaty. Others went to reservations because they felt they could do nothing else. Spotted Tail was one of the Indian chiefs who felt that his people had no choice but to go to reservations peacefully. He became chief of all the Indians at the Pine Ridge and Rosebud Agencies. Spotted Tail's nephew, Crazy Horse, thought that Spotted Tail was "selling out" to the white man. Crazy Horse refused to surrender and was stabbed to death when he resisted arrest. Spotted Tail mourned his nephew's death but continued to ask his people to accept their fate peacefully.

Spotted Tail (1833-1881)
(SMITHSONIAN INSTITUTION)

The massacre at Wounded Knee Creek (THE BETTMANN ARCHIVE)

After Sitting Bull was killed, a band of about three hundred
Indians — men, women, and children — fled in fear from the
Pine Ridge Reservation. They were frightened by the white
man's violence. No longer could they live by their old ways.
The fleeing band was surrounded by Government troops at
Wounded Knee Creek. The Indians surrendered. The
troops were disarming their captives when one Indian shot
his gun off by mistake. The troops responded with more
gunfire and a fight broke out. Almost all of the band, including their chief, Big Foot, were killed. Women and children
and many unarmed Indians were murdered in cold blood.
This massacre was the result of the widespread feeling held
then by the white troops that "the only good Indian is a dead
Indian."

RESERVATION LIFE

The Federal Government forced each defeated Indian tribe to live on reservations. Reservations were tax-free land "reserved for" the Indians. In 1871, Congress took over the allotment of Indian land. Under the Allotment Act of 1887, each Indian living on a reservation was given a certain amount of land. The Indian actually gained nothing because he had already lost over 26 million acres of land. In 1934 he had only 80,500 square miles left — mostly desert, mountain, or other undesirable areas. Government representatives were sent to the reservations to teach the Indians government policy. The Indians sent delegations to Washington every so often to ask for better treatment.

Indians receiving government yearly payments for their land (THE BETTMANN ARCHIVE)

A Government official addressing the Indians at a Grand Council (THE BETTMANN ARCHIVE)

A delegation of Indian chiefs visits with President Rutherford B. Hayes in the White House (THE BETTMANN ARCHIVE)

59

As more and more Indians were forced to live on reservations, the Indian agents became very powerful. These agents were often U.S. Army officers, who had at one time fought the Indians now living under their rule. Now the agents were in charge of keeping the Indians on the reservations and issuing rations. The Indians had once been proud and independent. They had been able to take care of their own needs. Now the reservation system forced them into idleness and powerlessness. The Government gave them rations because no longer were they able to hunt the buffalo and provide food for themselves. The food issued to them was so unlike what they had eaten before that many became sick with tuberculosis. Many Indians died from disease; others died from homesickness and despair.

Government agents distributing supplies to Indians (THE BETTMANN ARCHIVE)

Indians wait for issuing of beef rations at Jicarilla Agency, New Mexico
(AMERICAN MUSEUM OF NATURAL HISTORY)

Beef issue to Indians (STATE HISTORICAL SOCIETY, SOUTH DAKOTA)

An Arapaho reservation, 1870's (SMITHSONIAN INSTITUTION)

Indians on the reservations were very poor. Early crops failed because the Indians who had been great hunters felt that farming was women's work, not men's. They believed that they had traded their lands in exchange for Government support. But the food and clothing issued by the Government was inadequate.

During this period, reservation Indians continued to hold many of their sacred ceremonies. When the ground was dry the Zuni Pueblo performed dances, calling on the gods to bring forth rain. Sand paintings were done by the Navaho medicine man to cure illness. While he slowly sifted different-colored sands through his fingers, making designs with them on the ground, he sang ritual songs.

*Mother with sick child at sand-painting ceremony on a Navaho reservation,
Arizona* (AMERICAN MUSEUM OF NATURAL HISTORY)

The Rain Dance of the Zuni tribe, New Mexico, 1900 (SMITHSONIAN
INSTITUTION)

Now that the Indians had been conquered, people all over the world wanted to know more about them and their way of life. "Buffalo Bill" Cody's Wild West Show with its exhibits of frontier life was a great success in the eastern states and Europe. Everyone wanted to see the warbonnets, tomahawks, and wild riding warriors in action. Most of the Indians in the Wild West Show were from the Sioux tribe at Pine Ridge Reservation, South Dakota. They reenacted Indian raids against stagecoaches for cheering audiences. Cody made a fortune from this gigantic show but the Indians did not find it amusing.

Cody's original Wild West Show (THE BETTMANN ARCHIVE)

Chauncey Yellow Robe before entering Carlisle (left) and on leaving Carlisle (right)

Many Indians were sent to the first Indian school at Carlisle by the Government to learn how to live like the white man. When Chauncey Yellow Robe, a hereditary Sioux chief, entered Carlisle at the age of fifteen, he did not speak a word of English. He was ordered to cut off his long braids. The Sioux were very proud of their hair and it was their custom not to cut it unless a relative had died. These new orders and customs were frightening to Chauncey Yellow Robe and the other Indian students facing the white man's world for the first time. When Chauncey Yellow Robe graduated from Carlisle he went back to Indian schools to teach his people to see both the good of the old life and the good of the new. His contributions were noted by President Coolidge, who wrote a tribute to him when he died.

65

The author wearing a dress made of deer-skin, with her "modern" teddy bear, 1910

In the early 1900's the American Indians were caught between the old and the new world. The transition was very difficult for them. They tried to hold on to their own type of clothing and customs and their own economic and social system. Indians had been taught that material things and land belonged to everyone in the tribe. They did not believe in individual ownership of land or property. They believed in sharing. They also did not believe in the gathering and saving of wealth. The white man, on the other hand, who had first gotten his ideas from Europe, believed that property belonged to an individual, that money and materials should be saved, and that you sell goods in a business for profit.

A modern Navaho hogan. The Indians are dressed in blue jeans and dresses such as any farm family might wear.

Navaho visiting a sick child at Fort Defiance Hospital on a Navaho reservation in Arizona, 1954 (AMERICAN MUSEUM OF NATURAL HISTORY)

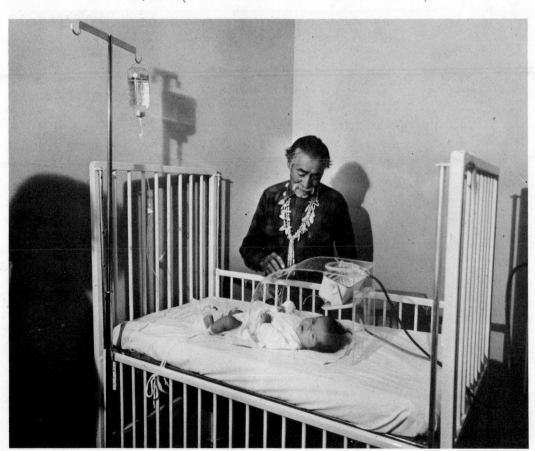

THE INDIAN IN THE MODERN AGE

The Indian Reorganization Act of 1934 gave Indian tribes the right to set up councils to run their own local governments and to handle tribal business. But in spite of this act, Indians continued to lose their lands. George Gillette, chairman of the Fort Berthold Indian Tribal Council, wept silently as he and other members of the council signed a contract in 1948 selling the best part of their land to the Government. They were forced to sign away about 155,000 acres of their richest farmland along the Missouri River. The land was used for the Garrison Dam and Reservoir in North Dakota.

George Gillette weeps as Indians sign away their land (WIDE WORLD PHOTOS)

Tonto and the Lone Ranger at a Madison Square Garden rodeo, 1951
(UNITED PRESS INTERNATIONAL)

Life on the reservations continued. Some people visited reservations as tourists, but most learned about the Indian from radio and television. Tonto, "the faithful Indian friend" of the Lone Ranger, became a household companion to many children in the 1950's. Tonto's real name was Jay Silverheels; he was a Mohawk Indian from Canada. The Indians do not like the one-sided picture of themselves presented on television and in the movies. They are often pictured as vicious warriors or unreliable, drunken savages who can only say "ugh." These fixed notions (stereotypes) harm the Indian in his attempt to get employment and education.

Many Indians have served in the armed forces in America's two world wars and in Korea, and are now serving in Vietnam. More Indians than any other racial group took part in World War I even though they were not citizens at that time. Citizenship was granted to the Indians in 1924. In both world wars the Sioux and the Navaho aided the Allied troops by sending messages in their own languages, which the enemy could not understand. Many Indian paratroopers were dropped behind enemy lines because they were such excellent scouts. In World War II, Ira Hayes, a Pima Indian, was one of the Marines who raised the American flag on Mount Suribachi, Iwo Jima.

Apache warrior Jim Lone Scout demonstrates Indian methods of scouting, 1937 (BUREAU OF INDIAN AFFAIRS)

Famous picture of the raising of the American flag on Mount Suribachi, Iwo Jima. One of the Marines was Ira Hayes, a Pima Indian. (WIDE WORLD PHOTOS)

Honored at a South Dakota Sioux meeting were two brothers of the Menard family. One is going to fight in the war in Vietnam and one just came back from Vietnam. (ROSEBUD SIOUX *Herald*)

Many Indians have become internationally famous. Maria Tall-chief, who was born on the Osage reservation in Oklahoma, became the prima ballerina with the New York City Ballet Company. She has danced in almost all the major cities in the world. Jim Thorpe, an Oklahoma Sauk and Fox Indian, brought fame to the Carlisle Indian School as a great all-around athlete. In 1950 an Associated Press poll of several hundred sportswriters voted him the greatest football player of the first half of the twentieth century. Will Rogers, who lived from 1879 to 1935, was part Cherokee. Known as "the cowboy philosopher," he became famous for his humorous comments on stage, in the movies, and on radio.

Maria Tallchief dancing in Tchaikovsky's Swan Lake (WIDE WORLD PHOTOS)

Jim Thorpe (UPI)

Statue of Will Rogers at Will Rogers Memorial, Oklahoma
(WILL ROGERS MEMORIAL COMMISSION)

Lieutenant Billy Mills sprints to a finish in the 10,000-meter race, 1964 Olympics (WIDE WORLD PHOTOS)

United States Marine Lieutenant Billy Mills, an Oglala Sioux from South Dakota, also became internationally known. He won the 10,000-meter race at the Olympics in Japan in 1964 and has broken several world records in track. Lieutenant Mills said that, as he stood on the pedestal being awarded the gold medal, his thoughts were of great pride that he was an American.

Also internationally acclaimed is Maria Martinez, a Pueblo Indian from San Ildefonso, New Mexico. Every large museum in the United States and Europe owns pieces of Maria's pottery. She and her late husband, Julian, rediscovered the ancient Indian method of making black-on-black pottery.

Maria Martinez, the famous potter of San Ildefonso pueblo, in northern New Mexico (NEW MEXICO STATE TOURIST BUREAU)

Chief Charles Bender's (second from left) skill as a baseball player first became known when he was on the Carlisle Indian School team. He went on to the major leagues and later became a member of baseball's Hall of Fame. (UNITED PRESS INTERNATIONAL)

Many Indians have become leaders in the fight for the rights and business interests of their people. Benjamin Reifel, a Brule Sioux, is the only Indian in the United States Congress. In the early 1950's Congressman Reifel urged that signs reading "no Indians allowed" be removed from the windows and walls of 33 stores in Alliance, Nebraska. The signs were taken down within the next few months. Congressman Reifel studied at Indian schools and public schools, and went on to receive his Ph.D. from Harvard. Another major Indian leader is Raymond Nakai, the chairman of the Navaho Tribal Council. Mr. Nakai speaks for the largest Indian tribe in the United States and has helped to set up a ten-million-dollar trust fund for Indian education.

Left to right: Rueben Robertson, Flandreau Sioux tribe; Cato W. Valandra, president of the Rosebud Sioux Tribal Council; Congressman Ben Reifel — on steps of U.S. Capitol

Raymond Nakai, chairman of the Navaho Tribal Council (BUREAU OF INDIAN AFFAIRS)

Navaho Indian Annie Wauneka in Secretary of the Interior Stewart L. Udall's office when she was presented with the Presidential Medal of Freedom, 1963. She has helped the Navaho learn how to cope with the dread disease of tuberculosis. (BUREAU OF INDIAN AFFAIRS)

Most Indians wish to preserve their culture and identity. The Philbrook Art Center in Tulsa, Oklahoma, was the first museum to exhibit the works of Indian artists. Because of Philbrook, American Indian art hangs in museums all over the world. At the Institute of American Indian Arts in Santa Fe, New Mexico, young Indian students from all over the country come to study the arts. About 350 pupils represent 85 different tribes. The tuition at the school is free. Students of the dance create their own modern dances, based on the Indian ceremonies of long ago.

Students at the Institute of American Indian Arts (BUREAU OF INDIAN AFFAIRS)

Winston Delormier, a Mohawk Indian, working on the New York Hilton at Rockefeller Center (LOOK MAGAZINE)

Today, the American Indian has found work in almost every area of employment. The Mohawk Indians of New York State are reputed to be the finest steelworkers in the world. Their job takes courage and training and they must serve a two-to-three-year apprenticeship. Most of the men in the Mohawk families — father, brothers, cousins, uncles — become steelworkers. Wherever you see tall buildings or very high bridges, a Mohawk is most likely working on them. Now the steelworking Mohawks live in Brooklyn, New York, near their union headquarters, and they have their own church with services in their native language. On weekends they travel back to the reservations and attend the great tribal festivals.

79

Bill Jones, whose Indian name is Soaring Eagle, is a worker at American Airlines (TULSA World)

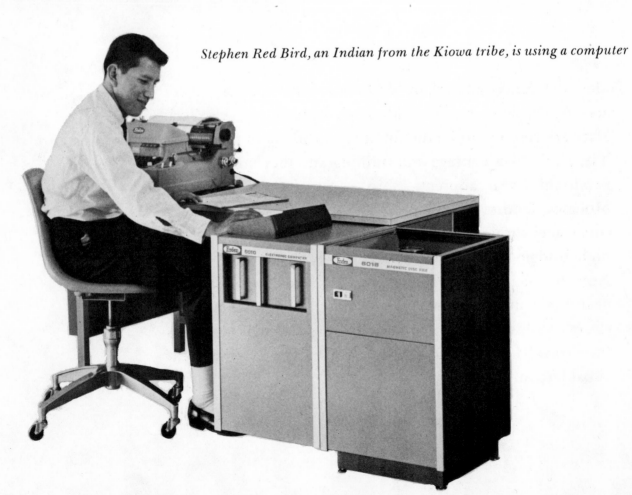

Stephen Red Bird, an Indian from the Kiowa tribe, is using a computer

St. Augustine's American Indian Center, Chicago, Illinois, 1966 (CLIFOTO)

Over 200,000 Indians have moved from reservations to cities
and towns in search of jobs since World War II. Very often
they were unprepared for city living and were very lonely.
In some large cities — Los Angeles, Chicago, Denver, and
others — and in some smaller towns, there are Indian centers
where help in getting jobs and housing may be found. The
centers also serve as social clubs where members dance and
visit with one another. Drumming and singing are usually
part of the social gatherings, whether in the city or on the
reservation.

Makeshift shelter, Rosebud Sioux Reservation, 1967 (GEORGE ENGLISH, JR.)

A few Indians in America are very wealthy; yet most continue to live in poverty. On reservations, Indians sometimes live in tents, shacks, and even old automobiles. Indians have the lowest income of any racial group in the United States. Over half of the Indian children in the United States have less than an eighth-grade education and most have no schooling at all. Educating the American Indian has long been a problem for the United States. The Government has made many mistakes. It set up boarding schools away from the reservations and took the Indian children away from their families and tribal life. Many of the children were very unhappy and could not learn. Education is improving on the reservations today with day schools and the Head Start program.

82

Children in a Head Start program at a reservation school in Red Shirt Village, South Dakota, 1965 (WIDE WORLD PHOTOS)

Only since 1960 has the Indian used picketing to express his views. These children are holding signs because their father, a Puyallup Indian, is in jail for violating state fishing laws. (WIDE WORLD PHOTOS)

Members of Indian delegation at the poor people's campaign, 1968 (WIDE WORLD PHOTOS)

The problem of Indian rights and identity continues today. In 1968, during the poor people's campaign in Washington, D.C., an Indian delegation protested a ruling which gave the state of Washington the right to control Indian fishing and which broke a treaty signed 101 years ago. Indian groups disagreed about supporting the poor people's campaign. The younger Indians feel that more picketing and protesting has to be done. The older members of the tribes believe in "person to person" talks. Yet all agree that the story of the Indian in the United States has been the story of broken agreements. Many continue to be troubled about the way they were treated in the past and the way they live in the present.

On March 6, 1968, President Lyndon B. Johnson sent to Congress the first Presidential message on American Indian affairs in our nation's history. The President said: "We must pledge to respect fully the dignity and the uniqueness of the Indian citizen. We must affirm the right of the first Americans to remain Indians while exercising their rights as Americans — their right to freedom and self determination. For the first among us must not be the last."

Chief Yellow Robe

GLOSSARY

CALUMET (kal'-u-met) A long-stemmed pipe, often called a peace pipe, used in many different ceremonies among the tribes. The bowl of the pipe was usually made of red stone.

CANOE A small boat, long and narrow and sharp at both ends, made of birch bark, wood, skins, or balsa. Paddles were made of wood.

CEREMONIAL DANCE CIRCLE A circle of dancers which was formed around singers and drummers in Indian ritual dances.

CHILKAT BLANKET A blanket with long fringes and designs representing animals, fish, or birds, woven by the Chilkat Indians, a division of the Tlingit.

CRADLEBOARD A thin rectangular board or weaving of flat sticks to a rectangular frame. Animal skins were lashed to the frame and an Indian baby would be completely encased in the skin cradle, with fur inside, and carried on his mother's back.

HEADDRESS A covering for the head. The different tribes made use of deer hair and antlers, fur, wood, copper, and buffalo horns for their headdresses.

KIVA (kee'-va) A circular room in a pueblo, used by the Indians for ceremonies or for social meetings.

LONGHOUSE A dwelling of the Iroquois tribes. Several families shared a longhouse.

MAIZE Indian corn, an important food for most of the tribes.

MEDICINE MAN A man who combined religion with healing. The medicine man was believed to have magic powers and the ability to communicate with the gods. The healing ceremonies differed among the various tribal groups.

MOCCASIN A soft heelless shoe made of animal skin and used by almost all the tribes. Two general types were used — a rawhide sole sewed to a skin or a sole and upper portion made of one piece of skin.

PADDLE A wooden oar with a broad blade used to move a canoe through the water. The Eskimo used a double paddle with a broad blade on each end of the oar.

PIKI (pee'-kee) A Southwest Indian bread made from a batter of cornmeal and water. The batter was spread on a hot stone and then rolled as it cooked.

POTLATCH A ceremony among tribes from Oregon to Alaska. During singing, dancing, and feasting, many gifts were given away.

SMOKE SIGNAL Made by building a fire of damp grass or wood so that it will smoke a lot. A blanket is thrown over the fire and then pulled off quickly to release a balloonlike puff of smoke. This puff of smoke communicates a message.

TEPEE (tee'-pee) A conelike tent made of skins stretched over a framework of poles. Can be taken down and set up again quickly and easily.

TLINGIT BASKET A finely woven basket of spruce roots used by a "stone boiler." Hot stones were dropped into a basket which held water and food. The food was cooked by the heat of the stones.

TOMAHAWK A small club used as a hand weapon, hatchet, or missile. Made of stone, wood, bone, flint, or animal horns.

TRAVOIS (trav-wa') (French) Two trailing poles attached to a horse or dog and bearing a platform for a load. Pulled by the horse or dog, the travois carried belongings, children, or sick people.

WAKAN TANKA (wakan — mysterious, tanka — great) A Dakota word meaning Great Mystery. The English use the words "Great Spirit."

WARBONNET Beautiful, flaring, eagle feather headdress worn by the Sioux.

WAR PAINT The Dakota people mixed blue, red, white, and black clay with powdered herbs. They painted their faces, their bodies, and even their horses with this mixture as a token of going to war.

WIGWAM An Algonkin dwelling used from Canada to North Carolina and formed of a framework of poles covered with bark, rush, mats, or hides.